Acknowledgements

We would like to thank the Department for Education and Skills (DfES) for their important contribution to this Guide, both in terms of funding and also their active support for its development.

Lynne Bryan and **Cheryl Turner**

Fuing

A guroups

Lynne

promoting adult learning

©2004 National Institute of Adult Continuing Education
(England and Wales)

21 De Montfort Street
Leicester
LE1 7GE

Company registration no. 2603322
Charity registration no. 1002775

NIACE has a broad remit to promote lifelong learning opportunities for adults. NIACE works to develop increased participation in education and training, particularly for those who do not have easy access because of class, gender, age, race, language and culture, learning difficulties or disabilities, or insufficient financial resources.

You can find NIACE online at www.niace.org.uk

Cataloguing in Publication Data
A CIP record of this title is available from the British Library.

Designed and typeset by Creative Associates.
Print and bound in the UK by Latimer Trend.
ISBN: 1 86201 196 6

Contents

1

Who is this Guide for?

This Guide is for smaller voluntary and community organisations that are applying for funding for neighbourhood learning. This includes groups that do not see learning as central to their work but as a step towards achieving other aims, such as enhancing the lives of their members, users and their local community. These groups may be less experienced in developing and delivering learning and in finding money for this purpose.

What does it offer?

Funding sources generally fall into three broad categories: public or statutory funding bodies, charities and foundations, and corporate funders. This Guide concentrates on statutory sources. These are Government funds that are usually allocated through central, regional or local Government departments and bodies such as the Department for Education and Skills (DfES), local authorities (LAs), the Learning and Skills Council (LSC) and Regional Development Agencies (RDAs). Intermediary organisations such as national umbrella bodies within the voluntary and community sector are also sometimes used to manage funding allocations.

The Guide begins by setting out some of the areas of learning that are potentially of interest to voluntary and community organisations, linking these to key areas of Government policy in order to help you make your case to funders. It then provides step-by-step advice on how to organise and write funding applications and points you towards organisations that can offer further support. It also refers to some major grant making trusts with an interest in learning.

Funding for neighbourhood learning is a dynamic area. New sources appear and priorities and application processes change. Consequently, some of the detail offered here may become out of date and key funds might be missing. It is important to check the possibilities before beginning an application and therefore the Guide also directs you to useful organisations, publications, websites and other resources that offer long-term support and up-to-date information.

2 Learning in voluntary and community groups

People learn all the time and in many ways – both informally and formally. It is estimated that between 70% and 90% of learning happens outside organised and formal educational activities. However, learning skills, gaining new knowledge, and thinking about things differently, can be strengthened and applied better if people are supported in their learning.

The Government has a strong vision of the importance of adult learning to the economic, social and cultural well being of the country.

"We must put in place a Framework that gives every young person a firm foundation and give adults opportunities to develop their skills throughout their working lives. But learning and skills are not just about work or economic goals. They are also about the pleasure of learning for its own sake, the dignity of self-improvement, the achievement of personal potential and fulfilment, and the creation of a better society."

The Skills Strategy, *21st Century Skills: Realising Our Potential Individuals, Employers, Nation,*
DfES (2003)

This potentially wider interpretation of the value of learning sits in the context of a strong and increasing emphasis on the need to build skills, particularly skills for employability, economic competitiveness, and literacy, numeracy, language and ICT skills. This is underpinned by a series of major targets around improving rates of entry into Modern Apprenticeships and higher education, enhancing basic skills, increasing the achievement of qualifications, and so on.

Being aware of this broader context for your work can be helpful. As a general rule, it helps to become familiar with the purposes, priorities and policies of potential funders. When applying for statutory funding for learning, it could be advantageous to have some understanding of

Government priorities and to refer to these in your bids, demonstrating how your work would contribute to their achievement.

"Applications are… expected to demonstrate clearly how they will help departments achieve their objectives. Too many applications seem to assume that the core work of the organisation is reason enough to secure government grant. I am afraid that no matter how effective or important the work of your organisation, you need to show how it meets the objectives of the funder."

John Marshall, Head of grants and funding policy, Active Community Unit, Home Office, *A Guide to Funding from Government Department and Agencies*, Directory of Social Change (2001)

It also helps to bear in mind that the Government views the voluntary and community sector as a key partner in developing and delivering learning. This reflects a wider appreciation of the contribution of the sector to major Government policy areas such as social cohesion, neighbourhood renewal, cultural diversity and citizenship.

Ways of learning

It might not be immediately obvious how voluntary and community groups with 'non-educational' purposes can become involved in adult learning. This is partly because learning can sometimes be quite hidden or 'embedded' in other activities and so we don't notice that it is taking place. We are concentrating on doing the 'job in hand' and not thinking about how we are able to do it. Nonetheless, when we want to improve the way we do things, or do something new, most of us need to learn something – new skills, new information, or new approaches and attitudes. For example, you may want to improve how you work with your client group, represent yourselves, campaign, or develop an entirely new area of activity. These will all incorporate some kind of learning.

The learning involved might be described as 'formal' or 'informal', depending on the approaches taken to developing and delivering it. Here are some examples.

Formal learning can include:

• training courses, which might be short or long, ranging from 'taster' type sessions of an hour or so to programmes lasting over many weeks or years;

- 'accredited' learning (learning with certificates awarded by an external body such as an Open College), which usually involve regular sessions over a number of weeks and some form of assessment process;

- competence-based training, where learners are asked to give evidence of their ability to do specific tasks leading to a certificate or a qualification like an NVQ;

- self-directed or distance learning, where people work through learning materials or a workbook.

Informal learning can include:

- mentoring, where learners are supported by more experienced people who can advise on appropriate ways to do something and help identify what's being achieved;

- coaching or shadowing, where learners work alongside people and learn through observation and trying out tasks for themselves;

- peer group learning, where groups of people share skills, knowledge and awareness and support each other;

- 'on the job' learning, where a group or an individual works through a task, perhaps discussing progress with others;

- 'embedded' learning, where the aim of the activity is something other than learning but in order to achieve it, an individual or group learns new skills, acquires new knowledge or confirms existing capabilities.

Areas of learning

The numerous different subjects people learn are often grouped together into wider categories or curriculum areas such as 'the arts', 'humanities' 'natural sciences' or, more recently, 'citizenship'. For the purposes of inspecting the quality of adult learning, the Government operates with 14 areas. While learning within voluntary and community groups is richly varied and not restricted to particular categories, there are some broad areas that seem particularly appropriate to the contribution of the sector to neighbourhood learning. These reflect key Government policy interests such as basic skills, social cohesion, neighbourhood renewal and citizenship where voluntary and community organisations are seen as having a distinctive contribution to make.

Numeracy, literacy and language support

Sometimes known as basic skills, improving adult literacy, language and numeracy skills is high in the Government's thinking. Planning for this area includes challenging targets – 1,500,000 people to improve their basic skills by 2007, measured by passing a national test. It is recognised that in real terms, this will mean engaging around 4,000,000 adults in learning literacy, language and numeracy skills.

The Adult Basic Skills Strategy Unit (ABSSU) has been created within the Department for Education and Skills (DfES) to steer work in this area and *Skills for Life* (2001) is the document setting out the goals and plans (see Useful Sources). The priority groups are:

*   unemployed people and benefit claimants;
*   prisoners and those supervised in the community;
*   public sector employees;
*   low-skilled people in employment; and
*   other groups at risk of exclusion.

Voluntary and community groups are seen as key partners in achieving this, particularly through their work with those who avoid more traditional provision and formal educational settings. This includes identifying and supporting the literacy, language and numeracy needs of group members, staff and service users. Groups can guide and refer people to other providers, offer 'taster' sessions or courses, support the 'hidden' learning of literacy or numeracy in other activities, or work with other organisations to put on courses within their neighbourhood. The Learning and Skills Council (LSC) (see Appendix A for an explanation of the LSC) has set aside £29 million for 2003-04 for capacity building to encourage work-based providers and the voluntary and community sector to play a bigger role in delivering *Skills for Life*.

Capacity building

While the term 'capacity building' is increasingly common, it can be interpreted in different ways. It applies to communities, organisations and groups, as well as to individuals. Broadly speaking, capacity building means ensuring that groups and individuals have the skills, knowledge and resources they need to realise their potential, to network and work together well, and to bring about desired changes in their environment, organisation, status, or goals. For example, this might be an important part of enabling residents to play an influential role in the regeneration of their estate or wider community.

Because voluntary and community organisations usually work close to the ground they are well placed to identify the capacity-building needs of their own communities and other local groups. They may also be well positioned to respond to those needs by developing and delivering the necessary learning.

For example, this might involve providing the skills and knowledge local people want in order to set up a residents' association or to represent the neighbourhood in a planning process affecting the area. Capacity building for local voluntary and community groups might mean developing the organisational skills of volunteers, managers or trustees to run projects or manage funds. Individual capacity building could involve supporting people in gaining the skills, knowledge and resources they need for a particular job and to progress to other opportunities (perhaps in further learning or employment).

Active citizenship

Active citizenship is another common term that can mean different things in different situations. It is sometimes used to describe being active in local democratic processes or representing peoples' views through other means, such as community associations. In its widest sense it describes the actions of people who work as volunteers or community activists, seeking to improve the lives of others outside their own family at local, national or global levels.

Voluntary and community groups are the places where many of us learn the skills and knowledge for active citizenship, such as working with others, campaigning, fundraising and advocacy. These are increasingly seen as valuable in themselves, and also potentially useful and transferable to other settings such as the work place.

Neighbourhood Renewal

The Government is committed to tackling the deep-rooted causes and consequences of poverty in the most deprived areas in the country. The National Strategy for Neighbourhood Renewal (NSNR) and its associated Action Plan set out government thinking in this area (see Useful Sources). Eighty-eight districts have been identified as notably worse and in need of concentrated attention and resources (see Appendix B). This is a 20-year strategy with the overall aim of ensuring that no one is disadvantaged by where they live.

The NSNR recognises that in order to succeed where earlier regeneration initiatives have failed, there is a need to deliver 'bottom-up' approaches to planning and action and to invest in the skills and knowledge of all those involved in neighbourhood renewal including residents, practitioners, professionals and policy makers.

The Neighbourhood Renewal Unit (NRU), located in the Office of the Deputy Prime Minister (ODPM), has the task of delivering the NSNR. The NRU has developed a skills and knowledge strategy setting out a range of actions, specific neighbourhood renewal funding sources, and a 'framework' for what it sees as the essential skills, knowledge and approaches for long-term community regeneration. 'The Learning Curve: Developing Skills and Knowledge for Neighbourhood Renewal' (2002), underlines the importance of involving voluntary and community organisations in developing learning for neighbourhood renewal (see Useful Sources). There are funds to achieve this (largely targeted at the 88 districts), notably the Community Empowerment Fund, the Neighbourhood Learning in Deprived Communities Fund and Community Chests (see Section 6).

The Government's recent Skills Strategy, *21st Century Skills: Realising our Potential*, also emphasises the importance of learning in this context, focusing strongly on the acquisition of skills as a means of breaking cycles of poverty and lack of work. It proposes the encouragement of 'learning communities' in order to connect learning through schools, colleges and more informal opportunities (for example, those provided by voluntary and community groups), and to enhance the capacity of communities to determine and grow their collective skills — *"By building learning communities we can develop the capacity of disadvantaged areas to create a better future for themselves."* Local Strategic Partnerships (LSPs), the LSC and Regional Development Agencies (RDAs) are charged with taking this approach forward.

Workforce development

The LSC has described workforce development as the

"activities which increase the knowledge skills and abilities of indivi
part in the workplace".

Overall, the voluntary and community sector employs around 2.2% of the UK workforce and it is estimated that voluntary activity is equivalent to about 1.5 million full-time jobs. Viewed in this way, voluntary and community organisations are an important part of what is sometimes called the Small and Medium Enterprise (SME) sector and their employees (and volunteers) need work-based learning and staff development opportunities in the same way as other workers.

Voluntary and community groups have a distinctive contribution to make to workforce development. As community-based organisations, they have the potential to offer coherent 'pathways' of appropriate learning in accessible and familiar locations which encourage people to move from more informal 'first steps' opportunities through to advanced level accredited and qualification-based programmes and apprenticeships. Guidelines and standards for voluntary and community sector staff training and development are being developed by the Voluntary Sector National Training Organisation (VSNTO).

Each local LSC (see Useful Contacts) has a workforce development plan and a budget to:

- support targeted activities that meet local employment and training priorities (but not as a substitute for employers' own responsibilities);
- set up links with activity supported by other budgets;
- support improved supply of training and learning by building capacity, improving quality and increasing flexibility and relevance;
- provide information and advice to individuals and employers.

This planning takes place in the context of a wider process intended to address the skills and employment needs of each Government region. The Regional Development Agencies (RDAs) take the lead in producing Frameworks for Regional Employment and Skills Action (FRESAs) with their key partners, the local LSCs, Job Centre Plus, local authorities, Government offices, the TUC and employers' representatives. The result is an action plan setting out regional priorities (including for skills training) and how each partner will address them.

miliarity with local LSC workforce development plans and the priorities and objectives in local

could be very helpful to groups seeking funding for staff development and training.

oluntary and community sector training consortia, RDAs, or government offices

ful information about the plans.

Groups can also play a role by surveying the learning needs of their workers and activists and planning how these could be met. Common areas of interest and concern include health and safety and first aid training, courses in management and communication skills, or training in ICT. If your group is an employer, contact your local LSC Workforce Development Team. You might be eligible for information and guidance including access to an advisor to help explore the available options.

Social issues

Social issues are a key focus of much voluntary and community sector activity and offer significant opportunities for informal and formal learning. For example, voluntary and community groups that work with ex-offenders and those at risk of offending have been very successful at developing constructive activities that build confidence, greater self- awareness and new skills. These could be taken further with the right support and resourcing. For example, it could be helpful to contact the adult and community learning team in the local authority and the local Crime and Disorder Reduction Partnership (CDRP). CDRPs bring together the police, local authorities and local people and are supported by Crime Reduction Teams in the Government Offices for the regions. They each produce a Crime and Disorder Strategy, set local targets and can receive funding for innovative projects in local communities through the Crime Reduction Programme.

Many voluntary and community groups also work in the area of drug misuse, for example, voluntary youth clubs that are involved in raising awareness of drug abuse, or groups offering confidence building, life skills and health awareness programmes. In this case, a next step could be to contact the local Drug Action Team which will have targets to cut levels of repeat offending and increase the participation of drug users in rehabilitation programmes.

Children, young people and family learning

Voluntary and community groups often develop as a result of work centred on local schools or children's activities such as after-school clubs and parent and toddler groups. These give rise to significant amounts of learning for the adults involved as well as the children. A number of Government initiatives can support this learning:

- the Excellence in Cities programme aims to improve achievement in schools, tackle truancy and school exclusion, and provide support outside the classroom for pupils at risk of exclusion;

- Sure Start programmes promote the health and well being of pre-school children;
- the Children's Fund invests in local programmes working with families and children of primary school age at risk of disadvantage.

Local LSCs also support a lot of family learning (including parenting education) and family programmes involving literacy, numeracy and ESOL.

Information and communication technology (ICT)

The Government is concerned about the emergence of a 'digital divide' (a divide between those who use and have ready access to ICT and those who do not) and its consequences in terms of social exclusion and economic competitiveness. As part of a strategy to address this, they have launched neighbourhood ICT centres – known as 'UK online centres' – which have the task of ensuring that all citizens are able to use the internet by 2005 by offering training and access to the technology. There are now over 6000 UK online centres in England. Around half of these are in public libraries and the rest are in voluntary and community organisations, colleges and schools (see www.dfes.gov.uk/ukonlinecentres). The Government has also supported the establishment of Ufl which markets online learning opportunities in nearly 2,000 centres through the branding of **learndirect**. In April 2003 Ufl took responsibility for supporting UK online centres (see www.ufi.com).

The Government's recent Skills Strategy (see Useful Sources) defined ICT as a new basic skill alongside literacy, language and numeracy skills. Many voluntary and community organisations have a strong track record in delivering ICT training and may have a significant role to play in delivering the resulting ICT curriculum as this develops.

The term 'electronic learning' or 'e-learning' covers a wide range of learning methods that employ electronic technology. This can range from using a data projector with powerpoint in a classroom to distance online learning where teachers and learners never meet. The LSC has set up the National Learning Network (NLN) to promote the use of e-learning in post 16 learning. The initiative to promote the NLN in adult and community learning (see Jargon Buster) is being promoted in partnership with appropriate providers such as local authorities and voluntary and community groups (see www.aclearn.net).

Information, Advice and Guidance (IAG)

There are important ways in which voluntary and community groups can support adult learning that do not involve delivering it. Offering information, advice and guidance (IAG) is a valuable means of helping learners. IAG is often undertaken by statutory organisations such as the Employment Service or Connexions and this can raise fears that the service will affect benefit claims and expose recipients to unwelcome bureaucracy.

Education providers are looking for new ways to inform, support and guide learners and particularly those within 'harder-to-reach' communities. Increasingly, this involves working with and through voluntary and community groups that have strong relationships with people who face barriers to learning and that could deliver outreach based IAG initiatives. Partnerships with established providers (such as the local authority or local college) can be a good way forward, bringing together knowledge of IAG and understanding of the learners and their circumstances.

3 Planning and preparation

Good planning and preparation are keys to fundraising success. They don't have to be time consuming but they do have to be timely in order for everything to be in place with the right people at the right moment. This section takes you through some approaches to this important phase of your thinking and although the suggestions are linked to raising money for learning, many of them are sound ways of developing other aspects of your work.

Strategic plan

Applying for funding should not alter the main direction and purposes of your group but in real life it can be easy to forget this when you are desperate for money. Stating clearly and publicly, through a strategic plan, who you are and what you do can help to prevent this drift. A clear statement of your aims and objectives will also explain more about your group to funders.

A strategic plan is usually produced by those most involved in running a group including workers, the management committee, volunteers and users. Plans usually include:

* **a mission or vision statement, or overall aim** – this might be only a couple of lines describing the long-term changes your group hopes to achieve, referring to the community or group of people you work with;

* **a list of objectives** – these are usually more detailed statements about the difference your group wants to make and might include such phrases as "*to increase*", "*to empower*", "*to enable*", "*to improve*" and so on. They will probably be both short and long term and should cover key priorities for the future. This could help your group to identify what areas you want to fundraise for.

Business and operational plans

Some funders may require you to provide a business plan covering the financial side of your group, especially if you are asking for substantial amounts of money. It is also likely that you will have to do some operational planning, or planning that organises how you will actually do the work.

A business plan usually covers a two- or three-year period and should outline how your group will achieve its aims and objectives. Parts of your strategic plan might be highlighted and expanded to explain your methods. A business plan should show that your work is sound in terms of your finances and capacity and therefore might include a budget with a forecast of income and expenditure.

An operational or project plan should cover your group's objectives and targets, the project's tasks and activities, a timetable, details of who will do each job, the resources you need and how these will be secured and used, a description of how you will monitor and evaluate progress, and a reference to what happens when the particular funding ends.

Monitoring and evaluation

It is worth saying a little more about monitoring and evaluation at this stage because these need to be in your project planning from the start. It is sometimes helpful to begin your thinking by asking yourself what success would look like for your project. How would you recognise it? How would you know it was there and prove this to others? This can lead to discussions about the signs or measures of success you would use, the evidence you need, and how you might collect it. This might be statistical, such as the number of people participating in or completing an activity (known as quantitative evidence or data), or it might be things people have said about the experience and what they have gained from their involvement (known as qualitative evidence).

Funders sometimes ask for monitoring and evaluation to be done in particular ways and they require you to follow their systems. So, before applying, think carefully about whether you are in a position to meet such requirements. For example, could you provide evidence of learners' progression into employment or further courses? In some circumstances, working with another organisation with established systems and sufficient capacity might be the best way for your group to provide the necessary information.

Equal opportunities

Similarly, equal opportunities issues should be part of your earliest planning. Increasingly, funders ask how you will make the proposed activities equally accessible and available to all. This is an important issue and one to think through regardless of external requirements. For example, if you are running courses, have you considered the timing of the sessions to take account of school times and terms, have you found out if childcare is needed, or free transport, if the venue is wheelchair accessible and local to the potential learners, whether the curriculum and staffing reflect cultural diversity appropriately, and if language support is needed?

Thinking longer-term or exit planning

Most funders are keen to know what will happen to the work at the end of their funding. This is sometimes referred to as exit planning or an exit strategy. You might want to continue the work of your project and it is unlikely you'll receive funding from the same source for more than one funding period. It is important to think through early in the planning stage how you will continue to support learners and develop the potential of your project when the immediate funding finishes.

Thinking longer term will help avoid missed deadlines and opportunities and crucially, it will reassure learners and other local people of the long-term presence of the work. This is particularly significant for neighbourhood learning in communities that have become deeply sceptical of the value of yet more short-term initiatives.

It helps to write down your priorities for the next 6 months as well as the next 2–4 years, your timetable for getting the money, and how your group will develop the necessary skills. This could be the beginning of a long-term approach to generating an income based on an action plan. This could cover:

- your group's mission or vision, and aims;
- a description of the project you want funding for (including its aims);
- evidence of the need for the project;
- a timetable for action;
- how the project will be managed (who will be involved and how they will do it);
- monitoring and evaluation;
- potential partners.

Collecting and keeping information

Keeping up-to-date information can save you time, stop you 're-inventing the wheel', and make sure your applications are as strong as possible. Setting up a few files (or databases if you have access to computer systems) can help.

Organisational file – this might include:

- the name of your group, when it started, who set it up, and why;
- an explanation of how your group is organised – by volunteers, staff, members, user involvement, who governs it (e.g. management committee or trustee board) and how far it reflects the people you are hoping to support;
- copies of your mission or vision statement, aims, objectives and any plans (strategic, business, operational);
- details of your constitution – charity/company limited by guarantee, and charity number;
- any policies including equal opportunities, health and safety, and insurance;
- notes on previous projects;
- audited accounts, if available, and bank account details;
- key contacts for fundraising activities.

Promotional file – this might include:

- a list of previous funders;
- a list of people who support your group in other ways ('in kind' resources such as accommodation, individual supporters and so on);
- statements from users or clients who have benefited from your work;
- press cuttings or media coverage;
- evidence of the need for your group's work such as facts and figures, case studies, photographs, and personal statements.

Information on past successes will help establish your credibility with funders who need to feel confident you will manage the money effectively. If your group has the appropriate skills and technology, you might consider setting up a website to disseminate and promote your work. This will also give funders an opportunity to browse through your information.

Funders File – this might include:

- a list of funders approached (with contact details), dates when bids were submitted, and details of outcomes;
- copies of any correspondence, including acknowledgements and thanks;
- a record of other information sent to funders to keep them up to date with your work - this is especially important for grant making foundations and trusts that like to be more involved;
- a shortlist of relevant funding streams (including statutory sources, grant making trusts, and local trusts and foundations) in your area.

4 Getting started

Making the right decision

Before you get on with finding the money you need, there are a few things to consider first which might save you time and resources in the long run. Working through the following questions will help.

Q. Is there really a need?

Voluntary and community groups are in a good position to spot and respond to learning needs. But are you sure? Sometimes we think people will take up opportunities but when it comes down to it, they don't. To make sure you are offering what people really want, think about how you identified the need in the first place. Did you listen to potential learners, check what they wanted and involve them in developing the idea?

Q. Are you best placed to meet the need?

Think carefully about whether you have the resources (time, skills, space, staff, facilities) to respond appropriately to the learning needs and ask yourself some hard questions. Is it worth going through a contracting process with a funder if you want to set up a short course for six people? You might decide on a different response. Is there another organisation (another voluntary group, the local authority, or the FE college) that could meet the demand equally well or better? Your role could be to highlight the need, steer the arrangements, guide and support the learners, or develop a partnership for a joint project.

Q. Do you have to go it alone?

Partnerships are important to the development and delivery of learning. For many (particularly statutory) funders there is an increasing emphasis upon contracting with partnerships that bring together complementary skills and resources. Being involved in these arrangements could mean you have access to research, information and help in applying for funds and delivering a project. For example, your Local Strategic Partnership (LSP), Learning Partnership, local LSC or local authority might have identified the same demand in their learning plans; the Employment Service might have statistics you could use to support your case; and the local voluntary and community sector umbrella organisation or consortium might help draft your application. Pooling skills and resources could achieve a better way forward.

It is also worthwhile remembering that positive experiences of learning often create a thirst for more and raise longer-term expectations. At some stage you might need to consider how to respond to these new ambitions and needs. Partnerships with other organisations could offer learners welcome opportunities for progression into further learning or other activities.

Developing the right approach

If you are satisfied that your group needs to go ahead with some fund raising for learning then taking the right approach to the task will influence the success not just of your application(s) but also how the work itself develops. Fundraising is part of an organisation's wider development and therefore it needs to reflect the nature of the group and its priorities as well as the needs of the proposed activity. Getting it right will vary according to the group, the circumstances, what is needed for the project, and so on, but here are a few general points to consider.

Involving everyone

It is useful for someone to lead on fundraising – perhaps a member of your management committee or a worker, if there is one. However, it is also important for your management committee or trustee board to have a commitment to it. Collective ownership of a project is important for a number of reasons:

- some group members might have political or ethical reasons for not approaching certain funders;
- discussion might reveal historical reasons for not approaching some funders – this could be particularly helpful if proper records have not been kept for previous fundraising;

- other members might have useful contacts who could help with the application;

- there may be good reasons for not seeking funding at a particular time, perhaps a more favourable source is on the horizon or circumstances will make it difficult for your group to manage the money;

- it helps to ensure the sustainability and continuity of the work.

Realistic timings

Generally, you need to plan and start your fundraising at least 6–12 months before any learning starts. If you are hoping to employ workers you should think further in advance and get into a cycle of planning up to two years ahead.

There are exceptions to this. Funders (for example your local LSC or local authority) sometimes have budget underspends that need to be allocated at short notice. Watch out for these opportunities but don't plan in the hope they will arise. Be ready in case!

Developing partnerships

Having suitable partners will have a direct impact on the nature and possible success of any bid and therefore the issue should be considered as part of your earliest planning. Partnerships are not always the easiest way to work and they require particular skills to help them function well, but at their best they bring together organisations and groups with complementary skills, experience, systems and, particularly in relation to the sector, access to excluded communities.

Working with other organisations can also make a project more viable. For example, a number of organisations, each with a small number of learners, could bring them together to make the learning more feasible educationally and also more fundable. A group might need to work with an organisation that holds appropriate quality marks, or can contribute child care facilities or systems to track learner progression. These might include larger voluntary and community organisations or sector consortia, colleges, local authorities or private sector training providers. Increasingly, voluntary and community groups are developing their own networks or learning consortia to share the tasks of delivering everything needed to support learners, meet funders' requirements and monitor and evaluate learning. Not all areas have consortia and where these exist, they differ in what they offer and how they function. Some are involved in strategic issues, some manage funds on behalf of local LSCs, and most have a role in building the capacity of voluntary and community groups to deliver learning and to engage with different funding streams for adult learning (see Useful Sources).

Partnerships are also helpful to 'exit planning' for the project. If key local education providers are aware of (and better still, committed to) your work, it increases the chances of building continued support for it into relevant planning processes.

Getting advice and support

There are many sources of information about funding and many organisations that can support groups in finding and using it. These sometimes offer developmental and planning support as well. Some areas are fortunate in having a dedicated funding advice worker or even a funding advice organisation to help with applications.

Information on funding sources is available from:

- publications on how to fundraise - many are published by the Directory of Social Change (see Useful Sources);
- directories of the leading grant making trusts, and corporate and statutory sources;
- websites and online support – *Funderfinder* is the most commonly known on-line funding guide but there are others (see Useful Sources);
- newsletters and websites for organisations with a role in supporting voluntary and community groups or learning providers (see Useful Sources).

Advice and support is available from:

- ***Voluntary and community sector umbrella organisations or local development agencies, sector consortia, regional networks and local authorities*** - local voluntary and community sector umbrella organisations or local development agencies exist in most local authority districts and often support groups in organisational planning and their funding applications. They have a variety of names including Councils for Voluntary Service (CVS), or voluntary action or community councils. Most are members of the National Association of Councils for Voluntary Service (NACVS) (see Useful Sources). CVS usually have libraries with funding guides and access to *Funderfinder*, as well as information on registering as a charity. They may also have a development or funding advice worker to support groups through the whole process and newsletters offering up-to-date information on local funders. They can refer groups to other organisations for advice around particular issues.

Voluntary and community sector networks exist in every government region in England and sometimes have workers who specialise in training and learning. Details are available from the NACVS website. They have limited capacity to support individual groups but could offer guidance on funding streams. Local authorities can also be a useful source of information about funding and sometimes offer support with fundraising through their community development workers. They may also have money for adult and community learning, and manage other Government and European funding streams.

- *Specialist organisations set up to help voluntary and community groups* - Funding Advice Bureaux can support groups around fundraising through information packs, funding forums and courses to build skills. Most offer a search facility to help groups select possible funders. There are specialist bodies and networks to help organisations within particular communities, for example, Black Regional Voluntary Sector Forums, bassac (British Association of Settlements and Social Action Centres), the Community Development Foundation (CDF), the Federation for Community Development Learning (FCDL), or local Development Trusts.

There are organisations that provide support to rural groups in particular, such as ruralnet/uk. This rural development charity offers online services to rural voluntary and community organisations in areas such as funding, sustainability and collaboration. 'Non-rural' bodies can also access their services through ruralnet/uk's partnerships with other networks including the Community Action Network (CAN), DirectSupport, and the Development Trust Association (see Useful Sources). In addition, Rural Community Councils (RCCs) offer similar support to CVS for groups in rural areas. They work at county level and details are available from ACRE, the national body (see Useful Sources).

And finally, don't forget that funders themselves will often give advice and information. This is primarily through their application documents but it is also sensible to contact them informally about your idea. This could clarify whether your application is appropriate (thus saving you and them time), and also other key issues such as funding limits, the availability of capital as well as revenue funding, how and when payments will be made, and auditing and repeating requirements.

Checklist

- Does the project fit your group's aims and objectives?
- Does everyone agree with the funding application?
- Does everyone understand why you are supporting/developing/delivering learning?
- Are you best placed to do this?
- Could you work more effectively in partnership with others?
- If you are part of a consortium or partnership, are you clear about your role and how responsibilities and resources will be divided?
- Have you used the support available?

Project budgeting

Statutory funding is usually short-term and concentrated on project delivery (rather than development). Few funders will give money soley for ongoing core costs such as rent, use of office and postage. However, as projects use these other resources, funding applications should include a realistic contribution to help cover them. These are usually expressed in the application budget as an additional percentage of the total to cover 'overheads'.

Costing

It is helpful to remember that costs are usually divided between:

- **capital costs** – usually one off items needed to deliver the project, such as building work, computer hardware or software, furniture, creche equipment, or flipchart stands;
- **revenue costs** – running costs for the project such as staffing, administration, consumable materials, publicity, travel, rent for premises, and staff training (for example, to use the computer);
- **overhead costs** – ongoing costs for the organisation such as heat, light and the telephone.

Funders may specify how they want the budget in your application to be presented but even if that is not the case, it is important to lay it out carefully. The usual format is a table, with costs given under appropriate headings such as teaching staff, meetings, creche staff, teaching equipment and materials, accommodation, transport and publicity (see table opposite).

Before you submit your application, ask someone to check your figures under each cost heading and your calculations and totals. Avoid including substantial amounts under vague headings such as 'sundries'. If these are included, they should be explained in a short note to follow the budget table. Ask for reasonable amounts – don't underestimate your time and costs but equally, don't seek unrealistically high sums.

If you are hoping to get funding from more than one source (sometimes referred to as 'match funding'), make this clear in your budget table and mention in a note when you expect the other contribution(s) to be secured. Some funders will not agree to their portion until they have this information.

If you are requesting money for a worker, remember to include all the costs of employing someone, such as recruitment, training, national insurance, pension contributions, management costs, increments, and annual pay rise.

Checklist

- Is your request in line with the funder(s)' normal range of grants?

- Have you gathered together all the necessary information about costs?

- Have you covered all your costs?

- Are your costs realistic and do your figures add up?

- Have you included a contribution (as a percentage of the total) to your group's core costs such as heating, lighting, telephone and administration?

- Does your application represent value for money?

- Have you sought a second opinion on the costings?

Project budget	April 02/March 03	April 03/March 04	Total	Other contributions
Publicity and recruitment costs Leaflets and Posters (Year 1: £600. Year 2: £600) Advertising including staff recruitment costs (Year 1: £850. Year 2: £500)	1450	1100	2550	Local authority:£1500p/a; Arts charity: £1500p/a
Support for participants Travel cost subsidy @ £3 per participant per week. Year 1: 25 participants x 10 wks = £750 Year 2: 30 participants x 10 wks = £900 Childcare Subsidy @ £7.50 per session to child minder Year 1: 20 sessions = £150; Year 2: 26 sessions = £200	900	1100	2000	
Capital Building improvements for new music resource (estimate available on request)	3000		3000	Regional Arts Lottery Programme £2,500
Equipment for teaching and learning Advent 7002. 1.8 GHz Pentium Processor (with music and video editing capability)	1500		1500	Youth Music Charity (for musical instruments) £2000
Learning Materials Books and Stationery	400	500	900	
Accreditation costs Year 1:21 Participants @ £12 Year 2:25 Participants @ £12	250	300	550	
Premises Rental costs for studio theatre and training spaces (@ 8% of total rent)	1200	1200	2400	Local authority: £1500p/a; Arts charity: £630p/a
Staff Salaries For teaching staff (paid on sessional basis) @ £16 per hour Year 1 = 810 hours Year 2 = 1060 hours. For non-teaching staff (assistant staff paid on sessional basis) @ £10 per hour. Year 1= 300 hours; Year 2 = 350 hours	16,000	20,500	36,500	
Staff travel and Subsistence Administration and office expenses. Postage costs estimated at £450 per year Phone costs estimated at £300 per year. Photocopying cost estimated at £250 per year. Admin. Staffing support (180 hours per year @ £10 per hour): £1800 per year	2800	2800	5600	Local authority: £3500p/a; Arts charity: £6300 p/a
Totals	27,500	27,500	55,000	28,300

5 Making an application

There are ways of approaching funding applications that will make the writing easier. Try to give yourself enough time (if possible!) to draft and redraft answers, letters and statements, and to allow someone else to read your application through. Break the writing into manageable chunks so that you can step back when you need to. And above all, keep in mind the value of what you want to do and how it fits with your larger aims – this will keep you going.

Some helpful dos and don'ts

Do:

- read the funder's documents carefully and relate your application back to their criteria, responding clearly and specifically to each one and, where appropriate, using their key words or phrases to emphasise the connections;
- make sure everyone involved knows the deadline for the application – late submissions are usually rejected;
- assume the application form is what counts - funders often won't consider bids that refer to information contained elsewhere;
- draft responses before writing anything on the form and stick to any word limits and boxes;
- complete the form in full – make it clear if questions are not applicable;
- type the form if you can, otherwise ensure everything is written legibly;
- ask someone to read the application through before submitting it;
- ask for feedback from the funder;
- thank the funder even if you are unsuccessful - you never know when you might need to contact them again;
- share your successes and failures with colleagues - this information makes a valuable contribution to the next funding application you or they might make.

Don't:

- send mailshots or circulars – they usually end up in the bin;
- make general appeals for funds;
- send lots of additional material unless funders say they want it;
- ask for unrealistically large amounts of money – it can irritate and suggest a lack of research or trustworthiness;
- make assumptions about the funder's knowledge of you or your work;
- recycle sections from earlier applications without checking and amending carefully - these are easy to spot and suggest a lack of commitment and thoroughness.

Checklist

It is important to check everything though carefully before sending in your application. This checklist will help you cover the important areas.

Funder's details

- Is your application addressed to the right person? Is it personalised (if possible) – for example 'Dear Ms Potts' rather than 'Dear Sir or Madame'?
- Have you used the most recent name and address for the funder and their contact person?

Style and presentation

- Does your project have a title?
- Is your application presented neatly and is it easy to read? Is the language clear, appropriate and without unexplained jargon or abbreviations?
- Is the budget presented clearly as a table, with figures listed under appropriate headings, and any (brief) explanatory notes given separately?
- If you are sending a letter, is it typed on headed paper, signed by the appropriate contact person, and does it include a summary of your organisation, the proposal, its benefits and outcomes, and the project budget?
- Is the tone positive and competent?
- Is it the right length or could you make it shorter? Remember, keep letters to two sides of A4 maximum.

Content

- Does your application say clearly who you are, what you do, the nature of your group, and how long you've been going?
- Have you included your group's name, address, phone number and fax, email and website (if you have one) and the status of the contact person?
- Have you described your legal and/or charitable status and included your charity number (if you have one)?
- Does your application outline the project proposal clearly, saying why the work is needed, what you need the money for, how much, and who will benefit?
- Does it include supportive detail such as appropriate facts and figures?
- If you are seeking match funding, have you mentioned the other funding sources, how much money is involved and when it should be available?
- Have you included an action plan for the project?
- Does your application reflect an equal opportunities approach?
- Have you explained how you will monitor and evaluate the work and demonstrate the outcomes?
- Have you described how the work might continue (if appropriate) once this grant ends?
- Have you included appropriate support materials? Remember, only send copies of accounts, annual reports, press cuttings and leaflets where this is appropriate.

Your records:

- Have you copied the application for your records and stored this appropriately?
- Have you reported back appropriately on the application and its outcomes to others in your organisation, your partners and other interested parties?

6 Funding sources

There are many potential sources of funding for neighbourhood learning. The most appropriate ones will depend on the nature of your group, who you work with, your geographical area, and what you want to achieve. The mechanisms for allocating funds vary between sources, between regions and even within regions and so it is advisable to take a bit of time to find out what is available in your area and how you access it. This section provides an overview of the key statutory sources for neighbourhood learning along with a few key charities and foundations known to support this area of work. Section 7 (Useful Sources) gives contact details for the organisations mentioned. See also 'Getting Advice and Support' (p.20)

The Learning and Skills Council (LSC)

The majority of Learning and Skills Council (LSC) funding (see also Appendix A) is for mainstream post-16 education and training activities and is allocated according to a funding formula. However, local LSCs have a responsibility to secure a broad range of adult learning, including learning for active citizenship and community capacity building. In addition to its main budgets, the LSC has more flexible funding sources that can support innovative community-based and more informal neighbourhood provision.

Neighbourhood Learning in Deprived Communities Fund (NLDCF)

The Neighbourhood Learning in Deprived Communities Fund (NLDCF) is distributed through local LSCs. In 2002/2003 it was restricted to the 33 local LSCs covering the 88 local authority areas eligible for the Neighbourhood Renewal Fund (NRF). The Operational Guidance for 2003/04 states that *"the scope has been widened to include other areas of deprivation that fall outside the Neighbourhood Renewal Fund Areas"*. The allocation has also been increased from £14 million (02/03) to £30 million for 03/04 (£10 million capital and £20 million recurrent or revenue funding). £3 million is allocated as 'core' funding, divided equally between the 47 local LSCs.

The purpose of the funding is:

"to support local voluntary and community sector organisations to develop their capacity to deliver learning opportunities for residents of disadvantaged neighbourhoods.

- *Enable local LSCs to make a full contribution to the National Strategy for Neighbourhood Renewal through community-based learning*
- *Improve the quality of the learning provider base, including the development of small and community and voluntary organisations, and the provision of neighbourhood renewal skills and knowledge*
- *Encourage the take up of learning opportunities, for example through the further development of Community Learning Chests."*

Operating Guidance: *Neighbourhood Learning in Deprived Communities 2002/03,*
The Learning and Skills Council

Revenue (recurrent) funding can be used to support a wide range of activities from encouraging innovative 'first step' learning in local communities to delivering literacy, numeracy and community leadership skills; from providing staff training for voluntary and community groups to mapping existing neighbourhood learning centres. Capital funding can be used to support direct delivery, improving existing premises, complementing other funds to establish a new learning centre, and securing ICT provision.

Local Intervention and Development Fund

The Local Intervention and Development Fund (LIDF)is available through local LSCs for local groups and organisations to support adult learning that would not be funded through mainstream LSC funding. This includes more innovative, informal and short-term community-based initiatives.

Regional Development Agencies (RDAs)

The Single Programme

The English Regional Development Agencies (RDAs) have been operating a Single Programme (more commonly known as the 'Single Pot') since April 2002. Different funding streams, including the Single Regeneration Budget (SRB), have been brought together to enable RDAs to support regional economic strategies and to achieve their targets around creating learning opportunities and sustaining employment. These strategies and plans will be outlined in the Framework for Regional Employment and Skills Action (FRESA) for each region.

Single Regeneration Budget (SRB)

The Single Regeneration Budget (SRB) was set up in 1994 (and ends in March 2007) to fund regeneration initiatives in England. Money was allocated through bidding rounds and under rounds 1–6, 900 schemes were approved worth £5.5 billion. Support is also aimed at environmental improvement and protection, crime reduction and promoting community safety. Although there are no further bidding rounds, there may be opportunities to participate in the 530 SRB schemes that are still active.

Skills Development Fund

The Skills Development Fund is administered by the RDAs and aims to support people in gaining workplace skills - from basic to higher-level skills. Some RDAs are establishing collaborative groups that will be responsible for developing priorities for action and for commissioning and seeking tenders for development projects and pilots.

Basic Employability Training

The Employment Service screens clients for basic skills needs and after an independent assessment, they can be referred for Basic Employability Training (BET). The scheme is aimed at adults with below entry level literacy or numeracy skills and it offers up to twenty six weeks of work-based learning. Bids to provide BET training can be accepted only from Employment Service approved providers. Details of the approval process can be obtained from your regional Employment Service or from their website (see Useful Sources).

Lottery funding (Community Fund)

There are six National Lottery distributing bodies. The one most relevant to neighbourhood learning is the **Community Fund** (formerly the National Lotteries Charities Board). Its main aim is to fund charities, voluntary and community groups and organisations helping to meet the needs of people at greatest disadvantage in society. Priorities vary between areas and application processes differ according to the size of grant. The minimum amount for applications is £500. The Community Fund is a consistent source of funding for opportunities to develop skills and knowledge within local communities. Organisations do not have to be registered as charities to apply but they do need a bank account with at least two signatories. There are plans for it to merge with the New Opportunities Fund – look out for a name change.

Awards for All is a lottery scheme aimed at local communities that gives grants of between £500 and £5000 in a simple and straightforward way. It supports projects that help people take part in community activities and which promote education, particularly to increase skills and creativity. You can apply at any time and will be told within three months if you are successful.

The Neighbourhood Support Fund

The Neighbourhood Support Fund (NSF) has several managing agents who are responsible collectively for around 650 community-based projects in 40 of the most deprived districts in England. It is targeted at young people aged 13–19 and aims to develop their confidence and skills so they can overcome barriers to learning and work. The programme finishes in September 2003.

Futurebuilders

This is a £125 million fund, led by the Treasury in consultation with the voluntary and community sector. It is spread over three years (2003–2006) to assist the sector in public service work. It has four key government public service priorities: health and social care; crime and social cohesion; education and learning; and support for children and young people. It will offer 80% capital investment and 20% revenue funding to be dispersed as a grant, a loan, or as an equity stake in a social enterprise.

At the time of writing, the outcomes of a Government consultation on the principles, targeting and management of the fund are not known. However, the proposals suggest that *futurebuilders* could support physical assets (building or office costs, reconfiguring a service, ICT), intangible assets (research into needs and potential, establishing evidence, sharing and learning about good practice), and development funding (investment in the development and testing of new ideas and new services).

73664

Local authorities

Local authority secured adult and community learning (ACL) (see Jargon Buster) is part of the range of post-16 education funded by the LSC. Local authorities often work with and through other organisations to provide ACL including local community groups, voluntary organisations, colleges and schools. Activities or provision can range from year-long courses to 'taster' sessions lasting an hour or two. Accreditation may be offered with these programmes but is not always appropriate, particularly for more informal, outreach and community-based initiatives.

Local authorities receive funding from the LSC on the basis of annual plans for adult learning. These set out the range of learning they intend to support and the organisations they will work with to secure it. Local authorities have their own procedures for consulting local people and providers and for setting priorities based on the needs identified. Community-based outreach workers (where they exist) play an important part in this process and would be an immediate point of contact with the adult education service if your group is interested in exploring and developing some ideas for learning.

New Deal for Communities (NDC)

New Deal for Communities (NDC) is one of the Government's flagship initiatives to regenerate some of England's most deprived communities. It is a ten-year strategy and so far £2 billion has been committed to 39 NDC areas. The Programme has five themes:

- tackling worklessness;
- improving health;
- tackling crime;
- raising educational achievement;
- improving housing and the physical environment.

NDC is delivered through partnerships formed between local people, community and voluntary organisations, public agencies, local authorities and businesses. If your group is in an NDC area, contact the local NDC partnership for advice and information about possible funding and to check whether your project fits the priorities of the NDC partnership delivery plan.

Neighbourhood Renewal Fund (NRF)

The Neighbourhood Renewal Fund (NRF) is intended to help local authorities and their partners improve core public services in the most deprived parts of the country (88 identified areas – see Appendix B). Funding is allocated on a per capita basis and the ID2000 indices of deprivation. Conditions attached include establishing a Local Strategic Partnership (LSP) and demonstrating progress towards achieving specified targets. Your local authority may be in receipt of NRF and be receptive to partners that can help ensure its effective use in meeting targets, improving service delivery and supporting community regeneration. It is available until 2006.

Community Empowerment Fund (CEF)

The Community Empowerment Fund (CEF) is currently targeted at voluntary and community groups in the 88 NRF areas and is intended to support their involvement in neighbourhood renewal through the development of Community Empowerment Networks (CENs). Lead voluntary and community organisations are responsible for administering the CEF which can be used to build networks, support outreach, surveys and training, and help community representation on LSPs. The list of lead organisations for each of the 88 areas can be found at www.neighbourhood.gov.uk/leadcef.asp?pageid=45

Community Chests

Community Chests are currently available in the 88 Districts eligible for NRF. They are administered by voluntary sector 'lead organisations' and offer small grants of up to £5,000 to community groups for neighbourhood renewal projects. Your local CVS, funding advice bureau or voluntary and community sector consortium could supply contact details for the 'lead organisation'. The fund focuses on the most deprived communities and can cover a broad range of activities that support learning, for example, a community festival or sports day, producing a newsletter, translating documents, covering room hire, or paying for basic ICT equipment or training. The funding guidance emphasises the need for arrangements to draw on existing knowledge and expertise and to work with organisations that have a good knowledge of community issues and needs.

Community Learning Chests have been combined with the Community Chests programme and are intended to provide residents with the skills they need to get involved in neighbourhood renewal.

NB *It is important to note that at the time of writing, the future of both the CEF and the Community Chests is subject to the outcome of a major review of community participation being undertaken by the Neighbourhood Renewal Unit. If you are interested in these sources, contact your local Local Strategic Partnership, VCS sector consortium, Community Empowerment Network, or local development agency such as CVS for up-to-date information (see Useful Sources).*

BT Community Connections

BT Community Connections is an award scheme that connects community groups across the UK to the internet. Since January 2002 over £1 million worth of internet-ready PCs has been awarded to more than 1,700 community groups. For more details see: www.btcommunityconnections.com/index.htm

Excellence in Cities (EiC)

Excellence in Cities (EiC) was set up to address the problems children face through living in city areas. It aims to raise their aspirations and achievements, tackle disaffection, social exclusion and truancy, and improve parents' confidence. EiC is implemented by local partnerships and focuses on individual pupils and their parents. The partnerships consist of all local secondary schools and the LEA.

Sure Start

Sure Start is a cornerstone of the Government's drive to tackle child poverty and social exclusion by improving the health and well-being of families and children before and from birth. It does this by:

- setting up local Sure Start programmes to improve services for families with children under four;
- spreading good practice learned from local programmes to everyone involved in providing services for young children.

Programmes concentrate on neighbourhoods with a high proportion of children living in poverty. By 2004, there will be 524 Sure Start programmes helping up to 400,000 children, including a third of under 4s living in poverty. Working with parents and parents-to-be, initiatives improve access to family support, advice on nurturing, health services, and early learning.

Children's Fund

The Children's Fund is targeted at 5–13 year olds and is part of the Government's effort to tackle disadvantage and inequality rooted in child poverty and social exclusion. It focuses on multi-agency working, bringing together preventative services offered by the voluntary, community and statutory sectors. The Fund supports adults in their parenting and with other issues including domestic violence, counselling, family support and health awareness. Funding is flexible and determined locally through local partnerships which decide, in consultation with community groups and children and young people, which projects to support in their area.

The Local Network Fund

The Local Network Fund provides grants from £250 to £7,000 for groups working with children and young people. It is delivered through an innovative partnership with the voluntary sector. A network of 44 local funds is managed by voluntary organisations, such as community foundations, with grant giving and community development expertise. Decisions are taken by panels of local people with an understanding of the issues faced by children and young people in their area.

The Phoenix Fund

The Phoenix Fund supports entrepreneurial activity in disadvantaged areas in order to generate jobs (and their associated benefits) in communities where crime and unemployment are high. It aims to develop the confidence, determination and skills of local people.

The Phoenix Development Fund encourages innovative ideas that promote enterprise in disadvantaged areas and in groups currently under-represented in business ownership. It supports experimentation, the development of appropriate skills, the evaluation of new ideas, and the identification and spread of best practice. Additional funding has been allocated for 2004–06 in order to:

- build on the achievements of Phoenix Development Fund projects;
- identify gaps in provision from previous bidding rounds (in terms of communities of interest, such as ex offenders, people with mental health difficulties and refugees);
- support sectoral interests, for example the retail sector and the caring industry;
- help geographic communities, for example areas of industrial decline or isolated coastal hinterlands;
- build capacity within intermediary organisations to deliver business support;
- pursue work with Business Link Operators and RDAs and others to 'mainstream' business support.

European funding

There are a number of European grants that groups can use to support neighbourhood learning. Some are managed by intermediary organisation within the UK whilst others are available through direct application.

The European Social Fund (ESF)

ESF is one of four major structural funds set up to reduce differences in living standards between European regions. It has three strands.

- **Objective one** is for economically disadvantaged areas. There are three in the country: the South Wales Valleys, Merseyside, and the Southwest region of Cornwall.
- **Objective two** is for areas adjusting to structural changes, for example, when a dominant industry is in decline.
- **Objective three** covers the rest of the country and there are five priority areas including promoting social cohesion and improving training, and supporting lifelong learning.

ESF funds a broad range of schemes and projects, including:

- vocational training;
- work experience and placement schemes;
- training for trainers;
- employment counselling and job search assistance;
- childcare facilities;
- schemes for developing or improving in-company training systems and structures;
- research projects that anticipate and help plan future workforce needs.

The application and distribution system for ESF is based on approved Co-Financing Organisations (CFOs). These include local LSCs. CFOs are expected to draw in match funds and to bid to the Government Office for the Region (GOR). They combine the match funds with ESF to contract with local providers. Some ESF funding is held back to enable organisations to bid directly to the GOR, or for organisations other than local LSCs to come forward to act as CFOs. Your local CVS, funding advice bureau, VCS sector consortium, local LSC or GOR will tell you which Objectives apply in your area and advise on the most appropriate ways of accessing resources.

Grundtvig

The Grundtvig programme aims to strengthen lifelong learning and funds a wide range of activities supporting innovation and the improved availability, accessibility and quality of educational provision for adults through European co-operation. It is directed at adults who wish to learn in order to:

- play an active role in society and develop their awareness of other cultures;
- improve their employability by acquiring or updating their skills;
- improve their ability to enter or re-enter formal education schemes.

The learning can be formal or informal and Grundtvig is open to all organisations involved in adult learning. Partnerships are welcomed.

Grant making trusts

Trusts are an important source of funding. In 1997, over 8,800 grant-making trusts and foundations in the UK (including the Lottery) gave £1.8 billion to charitable causes. Trusts usually concentrate their funding on:

- new ways of tackling problems;
- disadvantaged and minority groups that have trouble using ordinary services or are inadequately served by them;
- responses to new or newly discovered needs and problems;
- work that is hard to finance through conventional fund-raising;
- one-off purchases or projects, including research;
- short and medium term work which is likely to bring a long-term benefit and/or attract long-term funding from elsewhere.

Core funding is also possible for work that falls into one or more of these categories.

Based on *'Applying to a Charitable Trust or Foundation'*,
Association of Charitable Foundations website.

There are a number of major national grant making trusts. Here are three that have demonstrated an interest in supporting neighbourhood learning.

Esmée Fairbairn

Esmée Fairbairn is one of the largest grant-giving trusts in the UK. Two of its funding priorities are particularly applicable to neighbourhood learning. These are:

- social development – promoting community participation and self-help;

"We want to enable people to tackle social, personal, economic or cultural barriers themselves through initiatives which increase opportunities, lead to greater independence and give them more control over their own lives. We will fund work that gives them the right support, skills and facilities to do this. We welcome applications that actively involve people in making decisions that affect their communities, and where they are involved in planning, managing and reviewing their own work."

- education – adult education

"We support adult education where this combats earlier under-achievement or creates second chances, particularly schemes that give the hardest-to-reach adults the confidence, enthusiasm and means to re-engage with learning.

We look to fund imaginative, non-accredited and informal projects that are tailored to the needs of the most disadvantaged learners…giving priority to projects that are not part of statutory education provision and to those that do not already receive substantial funding from statutory education sources."

Lloyds TSB Foundation

The Lloyds TSB Foundation for England and Wales supports and works in partnership with charitable organisations, especially those working with people who are disadvantage or disabled. The Foundation funds two main areas: social and community needs; and education and training.

The second strand aims to enhance learning opportunities for people of all ages who are disadvantaged or who have disabilities. Examples of potential areas include:

- lifelong learning;
- literacy skills;
- pre-school education;
- promotion of life skills and independent living skills (particularly creating positive opportunities for disabled people);
- skills training for disabled people, including pre-vocational training;
- skills training for disadvantaged people, to enhance their potential to secure employment.

Nationwide Foundation

The Nationwide Foundation supports projects that demonstrate a clear focus on tackling disadvantage and deprivation and which fall within either rural communities or volunteering programmes. The former includes proposals involving education, training and support for people disadvantaged by their rural location.

Potential projects include community-based learning, transport and befriending schemes, activities to improve services and facilities in rural communities and initiatives tackling isolation by improving access to employment and the wider community. The Foundation also welcomes proposals for projects that involve people in volunteering for the benefit of disadvantaged groups, and opportunities for further education and employment training for volunteers.

7
Useful sources and contacts

Name, address and contact details	Website address/es
ACRE Somerford Court Somerford Road Cirencester Gloucestershire GL7 1TW Tel: 01285 653477 Email: acre@acre.org.uk	www.acre.org.uk
Active Community Unit Room 235 Horseferry House Dean Ryle Street London SW1P 2AW Tel: 020 7217 8400 Email: Public_enquiry.acu@homeoffice.gsi.gov.uk	www.homeoffice.gov.uk/inside/org/dob/ direct/acomu.html
Adult Basic Skills Strategy Unit Level 1 Caxton House Department for Education and Skills Tothill Street London SW1H 9NA Telephone: 020 7273 1223	www.dfes.gov.uk/readwriteplus
The Association of Charitable Foundations ACF, 2 Plough Yard Shoreditch High Street London EC2A 3LP anja@acf.org.uk	www.acf.org.uk

Most relevant publications/resources	Information
	ACRE is the national membership body for Rural Community Councils (RCCs). RCCs are a good contact if your group is based in a rural area
Compact on Relations between Government and the Voluntary and Community Sector in England (1998)	The ACU are currently piloting a website which will eventually detail all grants available to the voluntary and community sector from Government departments
Skills for Life (2001) *Skills for Life: A guide to funding adult literacy and numeracy learning programmes 2001-2002* (2001)	The readwriteplus website is especially good and presents details of funding sources
	Please note: ACF is primarily an information and support organisation for grant-making trusts and foundations. It does not make grants itself, and does not publish information beyond what is contained on their website. **It is unable to reply to requests from grant-seekers for advice or funding.**

Name, address and contact details	Website address/es
Awards for All Ground Floor St Nicholas Court 25-27 Castle Gate Nottingham NG1 7AR Tel: 0115 934 9350 Email: enquiries.england@awardsforall.org.uk	www.awardsforall.org.uk
Basic Skills Agency (BSA) Commonwealth House, 1-19 New Oxford Street, London WC1A 1NU Tel: 0207 405 4017 Email: enquiries@basic-skills.co.uk	www.basic-skills.co.uk
bassac (British Association of Settlements and Social Action Centres) Winchester House 11 Cranmer Road London SW9 6EJ Tel: 020 7735 1075 Email: info@bassac.org.uk	www.bassac.org.uk
Cabinet Office – Strategy Unit Strategy Unit 4th Floor Admiralty Arch The Mall London SW1A 2WH General Enquiries: strategy@cabinet-office.x.gsi.gov.uk Charities Information Bureau	www.strategy.gov.uk
The Charities Information Bureau 93 Lawefield Lane Wakefield West Yorkshire WF2 8SU Tel: 01924 239063 Email : funding@the-cib.demon.co.uk	www.cibfunding.org.uk

Most relevant publications/resources	Information
	Useful information via the web, plus details of regional contacts
	BSA works to ensure the existence of effective opportunities for children, young people and adults to strengthen their basic skills. The BSA has a wide range of useful publications
	bassac is a membership network of multi-purpose community organisations.
Private Action, Public Benefit – A review of the Charities and the Wider Not-for-Profit Sector (2002)	As this is a consultation document, the eventual legislative changes may be different to those proposed
	The CIB have a useful website that has links to other organisations. They are developing their service to be available in other parts of the country, and produce newsletters and advice sheets for voluntary and community groups

Name, address and contact details	Website address/es
Children and Young People's Unit Level 4E Caxton House 6-11 Tothill Street London SW1H 9NA Tel: 0870 000 2288 Enq: 020 7273 4906 E-mail: MAILBOX@cypu.gsi.gov.uk www.dfes.gov.uk	www.cypu.gov.uk/corporate/home.cfm
Community Fund St Vincent House 16 Suffolk Street London SW1Y 4NL Tel: 020 7747 5299 Enquiries: enquiries@community-fund.org.uk	www.community-fund.org.uk/index2.htm
Connexions Service National Unit Department for Education and Skills Moorfoot Sheffield S1 4PQ	www.connexions.gov.uk
Department for Education and Skills Sanctuary Buildings Great Smith Street London SW1P 3BT Public Enquiries: 0870 000 2288	www.dfes.gov.uk
Department for Trade and Industry: Small Business Service Kingsgate House 66-74 Victoria Street London SW1E 6SW Tel: 0845 600 9 006	www.sbs.gov.uk/default.php?page=/phoenix/default.php
Development Trusts Association 2-8 Scrutton Street, London EC2A 4RT Tel: 0845 458 8336 Email: info@dta.org.uk	www.dta.org.uk

Most relevant publications/resources	Information
	The Children and Young peoples unit co-ordinate the Children's fund and The Local Network Fund Visit the website for details of your local contacts
	Community Fund applications are available via the web, along with regional contact details
	The most relevant contact will be via your local Connexions service
The Learning Age (1998) Getting the Best from Each Other (2001) Success for all (2003) Getting Better Delivery. Guidance for Effective Working with Frontline Providers (2003) 21st Century Skills: Realising our potential (2003)	The DfES has several other offices around the country. Look up the relevant programme details to find which address is most appropriate for your needs
	The small business service leads on the Phoenix Development fund
	The DTA has a number of local members who are primarily involved in community regeneration. They are usually open to membership of other groups and may be able to give information on initiatives in your area

Name, address and contact details	Website address/es
Directory of Social Change **London office** Directory of Social Change 24 Stephenson Way London NW1 2DP Tel: 020 7391 4800 Email: info@dsc.org.uk **Liverpool office** Directory of Social Change Federation House Hope Street Liverpool L1 9BW Tel: 0151 708 0117 Email: north@dsc.org.uk	www.dsc.org.uk
DirectSupport	www.directsupport.org.uk
Employment Service	www.employmentservice.gov.uk
Esmée Fairbairn Foundation 11 Park Place London SW1A 1LP Tel: 020 7297 4700 Email: info@esmeefairbairn.org.uk	www.esmeefairbairn.org.uk
European Social Fund General information Co-financing	www.esfnews.org.uk www.esfnews.org.uk/co-financing/index.shtml
Excellence in Cities	www.standards.dfes.gov.uk/excellence
Funding Information North East (FINE) John Haswell House 8/9 Gladstone Terrace Gateshead Tyne and Wear NE8 4DY Tel: 0191 477 1253 E-mail: enquiries@fine.org.uk	www.fine.org.uk

Most relevant publications/resources	Information
A Guide to Funding from Government Department and Agencies (2001) *The Complete Fundraising Handbook, 4th edition* (2001) *The Guide to UK Company Giving 4th edition* (2002) *A Guide to the Major Trusts 2003/2004 - Volume 1, 9th edition* (2003) *Writing Better Fundraising Applications 3rd edition* (2002)	The Directory of Social Change (DSC) is probably the biggest publisher of directories of funders and guides to successful fundraising. Publication details are available from their website and publications catalogue. Some publications will be held for reference by your local development agency. DSC also runs a national training programme that includes courses on fundraising
	DirectSupport is a free advice and mentoring service, funded by the DfES, for community and voluntary sector UK online centres
	Most appropriate contacts for ESF and co-financing are local LSCs and Government Offices for the Regions
Excellence in Cities Launch Document (1999) *Schools extending excellence: Excellence in Cities annual report 2000-2001* (2002)	Find out about the local schemes in your area from the website
	FINE is a project of seven Councils for Voluntary Service (CVS) and Rural Community Councils (RCC) in the North East of England. It covers County Durham, Northumberland, Teesside and Tyne & Wear

Name, address and contact details	Website address/es
Lloyds TSB Foundation for England and Wales PO Box 140 St Mary's Court 20 St Mary at Hill London EC3R 8NA Tel: 020 7204 5276 Email: Guidelines@lloydstsbfoundations.org.uk	www.lloydstsbfoundations.org.uk
Local Learning Partnerships	www.lifelonglearning.co.uk
National Association of Councils for Voluntary Service (NACVS) Arundel Court 177 Arundel Street Sheffield S1 2NU Tel: 0114 278 6636	www.nacvs.org.uk
National Council for Voluntary Organisations (NCVO) Regent's Wharf 8 All Saints Street London N1 9RL Tel: 020 7713 6161 Helpdesk 0800 2 798 798 Email: ncvo@ncvo-vol.org.uk	www.ncvo-vol.org.uk
National Open College Network (NOCN) Kedleston Road Derby DE22 1GB Tel: 01332 591071 Email: nocn@nocn.org.uk	www.nocn.org.uk

Most relevant publications/resources	Information
Learning Partnerships Toolkit *Remit* (1999) *National Partnership Protocol* (1999)	
	The NACVS website offers a directory of all Councils for Voluntary Service (CVS) as well as other useful organisations. Contact NACVS to find your nearest CVS
	NCVO works with and for the voluntary sector in England by providing information, advice and support and by representing the views of the sector to government and policy-makers. NCVO has a dedicated website for regional information where you can find details of the black regional voluntary sector forums, and regional voluntary sector forums
	NOCN works to develop learning strategies that will enable people to succeed in learning, and in particular, to secure accreditation for their achievements Local OCNs can help groups to develop accredited learning

Name, address and contact details	Website address/es
National Rural Enterprise Centre Stoneleigh Park Warwickshire CV8 2RR Tel: 02476 690691 Freephone: 0800 026 0202	www.ruralnet.org.uk www.expertsonline.org.uk
The Nationwide Foundation (By telephone only) Tel: 01793 657183 Email: the.foundation@nationwide.co.uk	www.nationwidefoundation.org.uk
Neighbourhood Renewal Unit Office of the Deputy Prime Minister 3rd Floor, C/5 Eland House Bressenden Place London SW1E 5DU Email: neighbourhoodrenewal@odpm.gsi.gov.uk	www.neighbourhood.gov.uk/ndcomms.asp www.neighbourhood.gov.uk/commchest.asp? pageid=25 www.renewal.net
NIACE Renaissance House 20 Princess Road West Leicester LE1 6TP United Kingdom Tel: 0116 204 4200 0116 204 4201 e-mail: enquiries@niace.org.uk	www.niace.org.uk

Most relevant publications/resources	Information
	ruralnet/uk supports rural voluntary and community bodies via online advice services. 'Non-rural' organisations can access these through partner networks (e.g. DirectSupport). There is a fee to join which can be waived under some circumstances (e.g. for small organisations) Further advice on issues such as sustainability, funding, computers and communication and legal issues (originating from ruralnet/uk) is available to all voluntary and community organisations through 'expertsonline'
A New Commitment to Neighbourhood Renewal (2001) The Learning Curve: Developing Skills and Knowledge for Neighbourhood Renewal (2002)	Details of New Deal for Communities and the lead organisations for the areas covered by Community Chests are available from the NRU
Working Together, Learning and Skills Councils and the voluntary and community sector (2002) Learning for the future: neighbourhood renewal through adult and community learning (2003) Lifeline 1: Community Education and Neighbourhood Renewal (2002) Lifeline 3: Managing community projects for change (2002) Lifeline 8: Evaluating community projects (2003)	NIACE is the leading non-governmental organisation for adult learning in England and Wales. They have a wealth of experience in supporting the voluntary and community sector in delivering adult learning. There are a number of publications produced by NIACE that might help you, and their website also has information on funding sources The NIACE Lifelines series offers a comprehensive range of practitioner-based resources, addressing many aspects of developing and delivering community based adult learning.

Name, address and contact details	Website address/es
Office of the Deputy Prime Minister 26 Whitehall London SW1A 2WH Dover House Whitehall London SW1A 2AU Eland House Bressenden Place London SW1E 5DU Tel: 020 7944 4400 (Regional Development Agencies and Government Offices for the Regions)	www.opdm.gov.uk www.rcu.gov.uk/main.htm www.rdauk.org/rdauk
The Percent Club Business in the Community 137 Shepherdess Walk London N1 7RQ Tel: 020 7566 8729	www2.bitc.org.uk
South Yorkshire Funding Advice Bureau The Workstation 15 Paternoster Row Sheffield S1 2BX Tel: 0114 249 4343 email: enquiries@syfab.org.uk	www.shef.ac.uk/uni/projects/oip/syfab/about.htm
Sure Start Unit Level 2 , Caxton House Tothill Street London SW1H 9NA Tel: 020 7273 4830 Email: sure.start@dfee.gov.uk	www.surestart.gov.uk
Volunteer Development England (VDE) New Oxford House 16 Waterloo Street Birmingham B2 5UG Tel: 0121 633 4555 Email: info@vde.org.uk	www.vde.org.uk

Most relevant publications/resources	Information
	The Office of the Deputy Prime Minister (ODPM) is responsible for Government Offices for the Regions (GORs) and Regional Development Agencies (RDAs), as well as leading on policy affecting local government. Their website contains details for contacting GORs, RDAs and local authorities
	The Percent Club Index is a voluntary benchmark, measuring the contributions made by companies though cash donations, staff time, gifts in kind and management time, shown as a percentage of pre-tax profits.
	SYFAB has a range of useful information sheets available via the website. It is funded to give advice to groups in the South Yorkshire area.
Tomorrow's Future: Building A Strategy for Children and Young People (2001) *Creating Magic* (2002)	
	VDE hold details of local Volunteer Bureaux. These are useful contacts if you need help in supporting volunteering initiatives.

8 Jargon buster

This Guide (and potential funders) may use terms that are unfamiliar. Although these phrases or 'jargon' are explained in the text, some may still need clarifying. This 'jargon buster' aims to help.

Added value

This term carries a number of meanings: first, activities supported by funding which are additional to or more than those directly funded; second, the distinctive and particular contribution of an organisation or sector (for example, it is sometimes argued that the 'added value' of voluntary and community groups in the development of adult learning is their capacity to work very effectively with more disadvantaged and hesitant communities and learners); third, the scale of the difference (or the type of difference) for individual or groups of learners between how they were when they started learning and how they are once they have finished. The latter is sometimes referred to as 'distance travelled', and can also take account of the additional difficulties certain learners face in following the same subjects or courses as others.

Adult and community learning (ACL)

This includes the wide range of programmes offered by local authorities (from craft-based courses and learning for personal enrichment and fulfilment, to vocational and qualification-based programmes) and also the learning opportunities arranged by voluntary and community organisations. ACL also includes more informal community-based outreach work.

Benchmarks

Standards or levels against which similar achievements or activities can be assessed or measured in the future, allowing for comparisons about quality and performance over time and across providers and subjects.

Budget under spend

A budget surplus caused when actual expenditure falls below the amount specified in the budget. This often becomes available for reallocation at short notice towards the end of the financial year (before the end of March).

Capital costs

One-off purchases, normally of equipment or buildings.

Core costs

On-going running costs of an organisation such as accommodation, office equipment, administration, staff, heating, lighting and postage.

Depreciation

Loss of value (usually financial) overtime through wear and tear or through something becoming out of date.

DIY fundraising

Self-help fundraising such as jumble sales, collections or car-boot sales.

Embedded

Something that is built into or part of an activity and which might therefore be invisible or unacknowledged.

End date

The date by which a project or piece of work is due to finish.

Evaluation

Interpreting and judging the results of your work based on information (evidence) gathered through 'monitoring' (see below) with the intention of finding out if the original aims and objectives have been met, whether there have been unanticipated benefits and gains, and if there are lessons to be learned for the future. Evaluation involves more than just describing or recording an activity ("we organised a meeting attended by six people to write the bid"); it also involves thinking about and reflecting upon its importance and value ("the meeting was useful/disappointing because....").

Exit strategy

A plan addressing what might happen after the particular funding has finished, including how the work might be continued and developed (if appropriate). The intention is to finish properly leaving no loose ends and to allow for careful thought about future possibilities and expectations.

Funding cycles

The frequency or pattern with which funders invite and assess funding applications, usually within the financial year (beginning 1st April and ending 31st March).

Impact

The wider consequences of a piece of work that reach beyond its immediate outcomes. Impact might be experienced in another area entirely, for example an educational initiative might have an impact on learners' families and the wider community, or longer-term consequences for the local economy.

Income streams

Different sources of funding.

In kind

Support for your work other than money, for example equipment, accommodation or volunteers.

Inputs

The resources that go into a project.

Learning objectives

Specific goals or achievements set in advance of the learning. These are sometimes decided by individual or groups of learners, sometimes by the teacher, and frequently by both working together.

Learning outcomes

Results and achievements from learning by individual or groups of learners including outcomes that are planned (anticipated outcomes) and those that were unexpected (unanticipated outcomes). They can be specific and measurable such as improved qualifications or more intangible such as greater confidence and sense of self worth.

Legal status

In the context of funding applications, legal status usually refers to whether the applicant organisation is a charity, unincorporated group, or a company limited by guarantee.

Match funding

Funding for a proportion of the total cost of a project, usually with a condition that the funding to cover the remaining proportion(s) is raised.

Milestones

Key events, targets or dates that mark significant stages in the development and delivery of a project or other activity. These are often included in a project action plan (specifying who does what and when) as they help everyone involved to assess whether or not the work is moving forward appropriately.

Monitoring

Gathering information (evidence) in order to check and track progress. This is often in relation to particular 'performance indicators' (see below). Evidence might include statistics such as enrolment and attendance figures (quantitative), or learners' views gathered through feed-back (qualitative).

Needs analysis

Research into the needs and aspirations of a target group or community. This is usually a first or early phase in the development of a project.

Performance indicators

Pre-arranged measures against which progress can be checked and assessed as part of 'monitoring' and 'evaluation'.

Project appraisal

The assessment of a project proposal to see if it is worth funding.

Quality assurance

Ensuring that minimum standards of service and performance are achieved and improve. Recognising and recording 'learning outcomes' and undertaking 'monitoring' and 'evaluation' are usually part of quality assurance systems for adult learning.

Quality standards

Minimum standards of service or performance. These are often set and monitored by an external organisation and recognised by a quality mark.

Regeneration

Rebuilding areas and communities both economically and socially. The idea is at the heart of a major area of Government policy (set out in the National Strategy for Neighbourhood Renewal) intended to address the causes and consequences of long-term poverty, poor services, low public and private investment, prejudice and discrimination, and recognising that successful regeneration is founded on solutions that are determined and delivered locally (see p.6).

Revenue costs

On-going project costs such as rent, child care, transport, teachers' fees, and teaching materials.

Statutory

Services, organisations or funding delivered by central or local Government.

Sustainability

The capacity to continue and develop a project or activity into the longer term.

Targets

Measures of future achievement set either as goals to raise performance (such as the number of learners to have passed the national the basic skills test by 2007), known as 'aspirational targets', or as a minimum below which no performance should fall (these are a feature of the National Strategy for Neighbourhood Renewal), known as 'floor targets'.

Workforce

The collective name for the country's employed population or the employees in a particular organisation, service or sector.

Appendix A

Relevant Government Initiatives and Actions

Learning and Skills Councils (LSC)

To achieve its vision and rationalise the planning, funding and quality assurance arrangements for adult learning, the Government has set up the Learning and Skills Council (LSC). This is a national organisation, with 47 local arms (local LSCs), that aims to achieve greater consistency, coherence and accountability across adult learning whilst being responsive to local learning and training needs (see Useful Sources for contact details).

The LSC has responsibility for planning and funding all learning for people over the age of 16 with the exception of higher education (HE). Therefore its remit includes schools' sixth forms, Further Education (FE), workforce development and adult and community learning (ACL) (see Jargon Buster). The LSC is also charged with improving quality, widening participation in learning, and promoting equality and diversity.

The LSC's strategic plan to 2004 refers specifically to voluntary and community organisations as key partners. It is currently working on developing a clear operating relationship with voluntary and community bodies and this is reflected in local compacts and protocols and also work at national level on developing a national strategy for the LSC's engagement with the sector. There is a growing recognition that some learning opportunities, particularly for 'harder-to-reach' and more disadvantaged and excluded learners, can be developed and delivered best by working with voluntary and community groups.

The Compact

One of the Government's earliest undertakings with the sector was the development of a *Compact on Relations between Government and the Voluntary and Community Sector in England*,

(November 1998). This is a framework for effective partnerships between the Government and voluntary and community organisations.

The publication of the overarching framework was followed by a series of more detailed codes covering:

- black and minority ethnic voluntary and community organisations
- consultation and policy appraisal
- funding
- volunteering
- community groups.

The Compact is a guide to good practice and is not legally binding. Research shows that it has not been implemented fully across government. However, there are local compacts between local authorities and the sector, and a commitment to revitalising the idea nationally through the work of the Active Community Unit. Familiarity with the Funding Compact might be particularly useful in negotiations with the LSC and other funders.

The Crosscutting Treasury Review

This Treasury review of the sector's service delivery was intended to lead to new measures across Government to enable voluntary and community organisations to be independent and flourishing.

The Review report, *The role of the voluntary and community sector in service delivery: a cross cutting review* (see Useful Source), made important recommendations about capacity building, embedding the Compact, and arranging funding relationships. These include;

"There has been a widespread perception that so-called 'Treasury rules' are inflexible so, for example, no payments ahead of actual expenditure are possible. This perception is simply incorrect – in the latter case the principle is that no payment should be made in advance of need [Treasury emphasis]" (p.26)

and

"...there is no reason why service providers should not include the relevant portion of overhead costs [Treasury emphasis] within their bids for service contracts. These are part of the total costs of delivering a service" (p.25)

The Review has been helpful in explaining the particular contribution or 'added value' of the voluntary and community sector in the design, planning and delivery of services. This was located in:

- specialist knowledge, experience and/or skills
- particular ways of involving people in service delivery, whether as users or self help/ autonomous groups
- independence from existing and past structures/ models of service
- access to the wider community without institutional 'baggage'
- freedom and flexibility from institutional pressures.

Applied to learning, this could be interpreted as having the capability to:

- identify the needs of groups of learners who may be hard to reach
- understand how to involve learners and develop provision more appropriately
- be independent from mainstream adult education providers who may have failed to reach excluded communities of learners
- reach new learners and widen participation in learning, particularly amongst more hesitant and sceptical communities
- offer flexible provision that is responsive to very local need.

Private Action, Public Benefit

Private Action, Public Benefit – A review of the Charities and the Wider Not-for-Profit Sector (2002), by the Strategy Unit in the Cabinet Office, reviewed the regulatory framework for the voluntary and community sector. The aim was to address barriers that arose from outdated legislation.

The Review's main recommendations included:

- modernising charity law by updating and expanding the list of charitable purposes, enabling charities to campaign; and cutting red tape
- improving the range of legal forms available to charities and social enterprises for examples, by creating Community Interest Companies
- developing greater accountability and transparency by improving information available to the public and regulating fundraising more effectively.

In practice, this could make it easier for groups to obtain funds without becoming a charity and for trustees to limit their liability without having to become a Company Limited by Guarantee.

Getting the Best from Each Other

'Getting the Best from Each Other' was an inter-departmental Government initiative to support improved delivery of post-16 learning and training programmes and community-based programmes by providers working directly with learners, (including voluntary and community organisations). Their report, Getting better delivery: guidance for effective working with frontline providers offers a programme of '10 Steps to Getting Better Delivery'. The full list and report are available from the project website (see Useful Sources). Those most useful to discussions with funders are:

- Focus on outcomes – funding agreements should always take account of the desired outcome of the programme, and show how the outputs being provided relate to it
- Consultation – all programme development should be underpinned by appropriate consultation with Frontline Providers
- Access to funding and support for providers – funding bodies should make funding available in such a way that Frontline Providers are enabled to access funds to meet local needs, and build their capacity to deliver
- Full cost funding – funding bodies should ensure, as far as possible, that the delivery-price agreed with Frontline Providers on average reflects the full cost of delivery
- Timing of payments – funding bodies should look to time their payments in ways that help providers to deliver services
- Long-term funding – funding bodies should ensure that the standard period of funding for programmes should normally be not less than 2 years
- Lighter monitoring and control – funding bodies should aim, wherever possible, to apply the principle of proportionality and a 'light touch' approach in the management and control of funding.

Appendix B
Authorities eligible for Neighbourhood Renewal Fund

Allerdale

Ashfield

Barking and Dagenham

Barnsley

Barrow-in-Furness

Birmingham

Blackburn with Darwen

Blackpool

Bolsover

Bolton

Bradford

Brent

Brighton and Hove

Bristol, City of

Burnley

Camden

Coventry

Croydon

Derby

Derwentside

Doncaster

Dudley

Ealing

Easington

Enfield

Gateshead

Great Yarmouth

Greenwich

Hackney

Halton

Hammersmith and Fulham

Haringey

Hartlepool

Hastings

Hyndburn

Islington

Kensington and Chelsea

Kerrier

Kingston-upon-Hull

Kirklees

Knowsley

Lambeth

Leeds

Leicester

Lewisham

Lincoln

Liverpool

Luton

Manchester

Mansfield

Middlesbrough	Southampton
Newcastle upon Tyne	South Tyneside
Newham	Southwark
North Tyneside	St Helens
Nottingham	Stockton-on-Tees
Oldham	Stoke-on-Trent
Pendle	Sunderland
Penwith	Tameside
Plymouth	Tower Hamlets
Portsmouth	Wakefield
Preston	Walsall
Redcar and Cleveland	Waltham Forest
Rochdale	Wandsworth
Rotherham	Wansbeck
Salford	Wear Valley
Sandwell	Westminster
Sedgefield	Wigan
Sefton	Wirral
Sheffield	Wolverhampton